THE MORMON
Temple
Square

THE STORY BEHIND THE SCENERY

In 1847, Brigham Young declared, "Here we shall build a temple to our God."

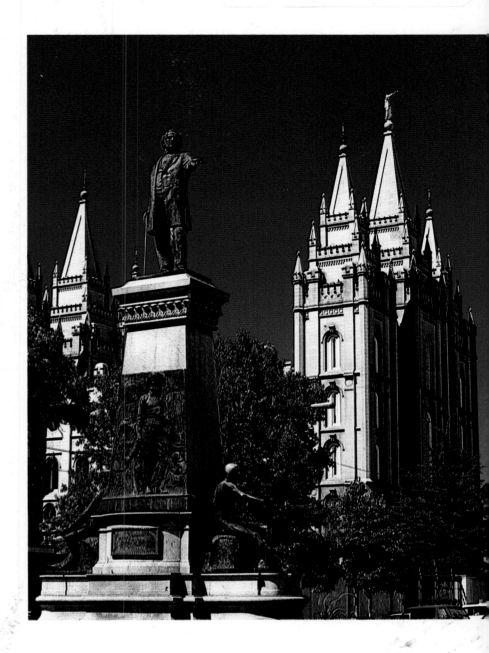

By Susan Easton Black

Dr. Susan Easton Black, a professor at Brigham Young University, is a recognized scholar in the early pioneer period of The Church of Jesus Christ of Latter-day Saints. She has authored over sixty books about the sacrifice, courage, and contributions of the early Mormon settlers.

Front cover: Aerial view of Temple Square, photo by Patrick Cone. Inside front cover: North Visitor Center and "The Christus" at night, photo by John P. George. Page 1: Brigham Young Monument and the Temple, photo by Rick McClain. Pages 2/3: The Temple at Christmas, photo by John P. George.

Edited by Mary L. Van Camp. Book design by K. C. DenDooven.

Second Printing, 1996

THE MORMON TEMPLE SQUARE: THE STORY BEHIND THE SCENERY.© 1993, KC PUBLICATIONS, INC.
LC 93-77026. ISBN 0-88714-076-9.

A feeling of thanksgiving permeates the Square during the Christmas season, creating a spirit of rejoicing, a time of reconciliation, a new beginning.

I prophesied that the Saints...would be driven to the Rocky Mountains, many would apostatize, others would be put to death by our persecutors or lose their lives in consequence of exposure or disease, and some...will live to go and assist in making settlements and build cities and see the Saints become a mighty people in the midst of the Rocky Mountains.

—Joseph Smith, August 6, 1842.

In the early nineteenth century in western New York religious revivalists shouted, "Lo here, lo there." The contest that ensued in the small town of Palmyra led young Joseph Smith to exclaim, "What is to be done? Who of all these parties are right; or. are they all wrong together? If any one of them be right, which is it, and how shall I know it?" One day while reading in the Epistle of James, first chapter and fifth verse, Joseph read, "If any of you lack wisdom, let him ask of God, that giveth to all men liberally and upbraideth not; and it shall be given him." Never did any passage of scripture come with more power to young Joseph than this verse. He desired wisdom and so on a beautiful clear day in the spring of 1820 he asked God in prayer.

The answer he received and the vision he saw of "two Personages, whose brightness and glory defy all description," brought joy to him. However, he soon discovered that by sharing his answer, he was treated with contempt and told all visions and revelations had "ceased with the apostles." Despite the ridicule and persecution which

JOHN P. GEORGE

The pioneers labored for forty years to build ▷
the Salt Lake Temple, a house of the Lord. This plaque, located on the exterior of the Temple, is a reminder of the hallowed nature of the building.

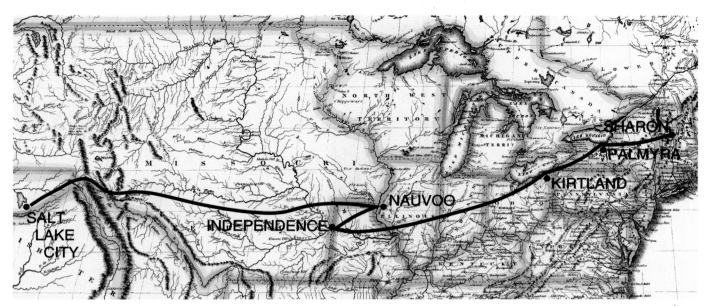

*T*he Mormon pioneers journeyed from Palmyra, New York, to Kirtland, Ohio, and then ▲ on to Missouri and Illinois. In each area they were seeking to establish a religious haven. In 1846, their quest led them 1,300 miles to the Salt Lake Valley. The saga of their sacrifice, persecution, and endurance is unparalleled in western history.

followed he continued to declare, "I had actually seen a light and in the midst of that light I saw two Personages, and they did in reality speak unto me...I knew it, and I knew that God knew it, and I could not deny it."

Three and a half years after the first vision, Angel Moroni—an ancient prophet who had once lived in America—appeared to Joseph Smith. The angel told him of a book "written upon gold plates giving an account of the former inhabitants of this continent." In 1829, Joseph was privileged to translate the ancient writings, known as the Book of Mormon. The contents of this book were shared with family, friends, and newfound acquaintances from New England to the frontier of the United States. Believers embraced its truths and viewed it as a companion scripture to the Bible.

On April 6, 1830, a few believers gathered in Fayette, New York, to organize a church, today known as The Church of Jesus Christ of Latter-day Saints. From small beginnings the Church grew rapidly despite mounting persecution in New York, Ohio, and Missouri. Amid conflict, even an extermination order issued by the state of Missouri, the Church continued to grow by thousands as missionaries shared the Book of Mormon on this continent and in the British Isles.

By 1839, members flocked to the swamplands of Illinois, where they enjoyed a season of peace, and built the beautiful city, Nauvoo. As visitors and converts arrived daily in Nauvoo they often sought an audience with the Prophet. One of the most distinguished men was Josiah Quincy, a former mayor of Boston. Mr. Quincy wrote of Joseph Smith, "It is by no means improbable that some future textbook...will contain a question something like this: What historical American of the nineteenth century has exerted the most powerful influence upon the destinies of his countrymen? And it is by no means impossible that the answer to the interrogatory may be thus written: Joseph Smith, the Mormon Prophet...."

To the sorrow of the Mormons, Joseph Smith was brutally murdered on June 27, 1844, in Carthage, Illinois. After his martyrdom, Brigham Young led Church members from the borders of the United States to safety in the Rocky Mountains. The story of their flight from Nauvoo to the desert of the Salt Lake Valley is an epic of courage and sacrifice unmatched in western history.

Four days after their arrival in the valley, Brigham Young proposed the building of a Salt Lake Temple.

*He instructed the pioneers
to begin anew for,
"I want to see the Temple
built in a manner that it will endure
through the Millennium."*

The Temple

The invitation to "Come, Come ye Saints" beckons millions to Temple Square in the valley of the Great Salt Lake. On Temple Square, a house of the Lord, a temple to God rises majestically heavenward as a symbol of pioneer industry, fortitude, and devotion.

Four days after the first Mormon pioneer company entered the Salt Lake Valley in 1847, Brigham Young struck his cane to the ground where the Temple now stands and declared, "Here we shall build a temple to our God."

Young selected architect Truman O. Angell, Sr., to draw the plans for the Temple. "I labored as hard as any man could," Angell wrote, "It is a trifle to labor with one's own hands to the labor of the mind. While one tires the extremities the other

NO 12
ERECTED   JUNE 12, 1932
GREAT SALT LAKE
BASE AND MERIDIAN
LATITUDE 40°46'04"—LONGITUDE 111°54'00"
ALTITUDE (SIDEWALK) 4327.27 FT.
FIXED BY ORSON PRATT ASSISTED BY HENRY G. SHERWOOD,
AUGUST 3, 1847, WHEN BEGINNING THE ORIGINAL SURVEY OF
"GREAT SALT LAKE CITY," AROUND THE "MORMON" TEMPLE SITE
DESIGNATED BY BRIGHAM YOUNG JULY 28, 1847. THE CITY STREETS
WERE NAMED AND NUMBERED FROM THIS POINT.

JOHN P. GEORGE

▲ *The Meridian Marker designates the geographical site where pioneers, Orson Pratt and Henry Sherwood, began surveying the plot for Salt Lake City. Since their assessment, Temple Square has been viewed as the center of the Salt Lake Valley.*

wearies the man in his whole system." As Angell continued to refine the architectural drawings, on February 14, 1853, the frozen ground was broken by Brigham Young's first shovel of desert soil.

The First Foundation

The original foundation of the Temple was made of red sandstone quarried in the Red Butte Canyon northeast of Salt Lake City. Workers hacked against stone that broke their crude tools and exhausted the unskilled masons. Despite the hardships imposed by this pioneering venture, by 1855 the massive foundation, laid 16 feet below ground level, was finished.

As work progressed, the United States Army, under presidential order to quell libelous rumors of sedition, threatened to invade the Salt Lake Valley. Brigham Young declared, "This band of marauders would win for themselves nothing but charred homes and chopped down trees." In response to his determined pledge, the pioneers filled their homes with straw and hay in readiness to torch personal property, but hesitated to destroy their labors on the Temple. The Temple foundation and important Church documents were buried under mounds of dirt that were smoothed over to resemble a freshly plowed field. Young offered a prayer of protection on August 13, 1857, petitioning the Lord for "power to finish this Temple even to the top stone."

When the threat of war subsided in 1860 the pioneer laborers unearthed the Temple foundation. Upon close inspection Brigham Young observed that the stones were "not laid solid, but were laid on chinking, small stones," concluding, "they would not support the great temple." He

▲ ***A* temple to God rises majestically** *heavenward as a symbol of pioneer industry, fortitude, and devotion. Building with enduring granite was an energetic undertaking by the Mormon settlers, but the edifice they built is not only imposing in size but architecturally impressive. Large derricks were used to hoist the hand-hewn stones to the tallest spires—a labor of sacrifice and love.*

instructed the pioneers to begin anew for, "I want to see the Temple built in a manner that it will endure through the Millennium." The crumbling sandstone was discarded for the more enduring granite found in Little Cottonwood Canyon, about 23 miles southeast of Salt Lake City.

STONES FOR A NEW FOUNDATION

Mining the granite was an energetic undertaking. Pioneers drilled a series of holes about

Stone masons labored to claim granite
boulders from the mountainside. The work was hard and not without its hazards, but it progressed rapidly as they worked in unison to complete the arduous task.

four inches deep every seven inches along the grain of the mountain. When the holes formed a dotted line across the length of the massive rock, wedges were driven and a rhythmic pounding from one wedge to another began. Gigantic boulders entombed in the mountainside responded to the pounding by hurling to the ground below. One such boulder provided 2,960 stones that weighed about 2,500 pounds each. Thus the pioneers transformed the rough cathedrals of nature into Temple building blocks.

Annie Wells Cannon remembered the first Temple stones brought to the Square in 1860: "The sight of the great stones one at a time being hauled along the streets by two yoke of oxen [caused all to] stand for them to pass with a feeling of awe and reverence." Large derricks were used to place the stones on the Temple walls. The process was slow and the task arduous, yet the pioneers patiently labored for forty years.

They built the Temple walls nine feet thick at ground level and six feet thick at the top. After hoisting the final stones to the pinnacle of the tallest spire, masons began to create fine etchings

The gigantic stones were dragged to Temple Square by yokes of oxen. At the Square they were hewn by stone masons to fit perfectly one on top of the other before becoming part of the Temple wall. This historic photograph of the partially completed Salt Lake Temple reveals the laborers, their pioneering tools, and the edifice they sought for forty years to complete.

▲ **The legacy of constructing Temple Square** *and the surrounding area is more than a heritage of architects and builders, it is an epic filled with vision, faith, and courage. The diorama reveals other interesting buildings outside of the Square: the Lion House, the Beehive House, a museum, a family history center, and the Eagle Gate monument are but a few.*

in the granite symbolic of celestial vistas. Fifty moonstones depicting the 1878 lunar cycle, the Big and Little Dippers, stars, and sunstones were carved into the stone.

CREATING SYMBOLIC ADORNMENTS

Pioneer artisans studying in Paris, France, returned to the Salt Lake Valley to adorn the interior of the Temple. Under inspired direction they created symbolic illustrations depicting aspects of the holy temple ordinances. Other talented settlers crafted fine wood carvings, made delicate lace draperies, and created exquisite silk curtains. The grandeur of the interior they created from the marble inlaid floors and carved fonts to the frescoed ceilings blends to perfection a monument of pioneer ingenuity, creativity and, most of all, devotion.

Skilled ▷
stonemasons created carvings symbolic of celestial vistas. Stones depicting the earth, the moon, the sun, and the stars are carved into the Temple's

exterior. These were created to represent "Celestial bodies...one glory of the sun, and another glory of the moon, and another glory of the stars" (First Corinthians 15:40-41).

▲ **As long as the Salt Lake Temple** stands, the name of architect, Truman O. Angell, will be held in grateful remembrance for his talented contribution.

The final and most eye-catching creation of the Temple was made by the renowned sculptor, Cyrus E. Dallin. He sculpted a statue of Angel Moroni, the last ancient American prophet to write in the Book of Mormon. His statue is symbolic of the prophecy, "And I saw another angel fly in the midst of heaven, having the everlasting gospel to preach unto them that dwell on the earth" (Revelation 14:6). Dallin's model of the angel was sent to Ohio, where its mold was hammered from copper and covered with 22-carat gold. The Angel Moroni now symbolically trumpets the gospel from atop the 210-foot central east spire.

DEDICATION OF THE COMPLETED TEMPLE

By April 6, 1893, construction on the Salt Lake Temple was complete. Thousands of pioneers from settlements throughout the Rocky Mountains gathered in the Salt Lake Valley hoping to attend the dedication ceremony of the great Temple. They were greeted with snow and a "wind velocity of sixty miles per hour." Despite the inclement weather they stood patiently waiting for the Temple doors to open and to be ushered into the beautiful, gold-trimmed assembly room. This room, like all rooms, alcoves, and halls in the

Temple surpassed the beauty and grandeur anticipated by those present. Their reverential awe for the Temple seemed to create a catalyst to a season of rejoicing, a time of reconciliation, and a new beginning.

One attendee who literally felt a sense of newness was Emma Bennett, who gave birth to a son during the dedication ceremony of the Temple. Eight days afterward, she and her husband and infant returned to Temple Square seeking a blessing. In the blessing her son was given the name Joseph Temple Bennett.

The story of this young baby and his parents symbolizes the relationship between a family and the Temple. In the Temple the greatest joys—the beautiful relationships between husband and wife and parent and child—become eternal. For Latter-day Saints the Temple is a sacred edifice in which the mysteries of life are explained in eternal symbolism. Solemn questions of "Where did I come from?" "Why am I here?" "Where am I going?" and "Is there life after death?" are answered.

THE TEMPLE IS SACRED

As the Temple is sacred, so are the ordinances performed therein. Because of the sacred nature of the Temple, visitors are not invited to tour the interior of the building. However, the quiet and serene spirit of the Salt Lake Temple, hallowed by the sacred work performed within, make it an unforgettable sight for every visitor.

The cost of the edifice was just under three and a half million dollars, but the cost in pioneer sacrifice "will never be known until eternity shall reveal the secrets of this life." The monument the pioneers built is a house of the Lord. It stands as a symbol of their stalwart faith.

SUGGESTED READING

PACKER, BOYD K. *The Holy Temple.* Salt Lake City, Utah: Bookcraft, 1980.

TALMAGE, JAMES E. *The House of the Lord.* Salt Lake City, Utah: Deseret Book Company, 1971.

The Temple is symbolic of purity, peace, ▷ and oneness with God. During most seasons it is surrounded by colorful flowers. Visitors agree that the impressive edifice is most beautiful in the spring, when the blossoms begin to reach their full bloom. The array of flowers, clustered against the lofty vertical lines of the Temple, is an unforgettable sight.

HARRY JARVIS

▲ **The gardens that surround the Salt Lake Temple are filled with unusual** and varied flowers, shrubbery, and trees. Nearly 500 varieties of seasonal flowers are planted each year, and over 130,000 plants are grown every six months in greenhouses before being planted in the manicured gardens near the Temple. The botanical delight created by the landscaped design is as "eye-catching" as the building itself.

▲ **N**ightfall at Temple Square is never more beautiful than during the Christmas holiday season. Some claim it is the expressions of joy and happiness of the visitors, while others profess it to be the colored lights, the concert series, the Christmas carols, and the manger scene. The spirit of the holiday permeates old and young, rich and poor, the hopeful and the downtrodden as each remembers, "For unto you is born this day in the city of David a Saviour, which is Christ the Lord" (Luke 2:11). The birth of Jesus, the babe in the manger, brings hope to all.

***A* quiet, serene spirit fills the Square** ◢
at night as gates close to await the dawning
of a new day. Disturbing the solemn
darkness of the midnight sky is the moon as
it shines amid the Temple spires. The
dramatic effect captured by the camera is
often lost by those who slumber.

◀ ***T*he ornate designs on the bronze**
Temple doors are typical of the exquisite
carvings found on the exterior of the building.
The designs are also representative of the
detailed nature of the Temple's interior. From
the marble inlaid floors and carved fonts to
the frescoed ceilings, the interior blends
to perfection the artistic skills
of the pioneers.

◀ **O**n the east center tower is a statue of Angel Moroni. Cyrus E. Dallin, an acclaimed sculptor, created the statue of Moroni, an ancient American prophet who was the last writer in the Book of Mormon. Members of The Church of Jesus Christ of Latter-day Saints consider the Book of Mormon a companion scripture to the Bible. The statue is symbolic of the prophecy of John the Revelator, "And I saw another angel fly in the midst of heaven, having the everlasting gospel to preach unto them that dwell on the earth, and to every nation, and kindred, and tongue, and people" (Revelation 14:6). It is made of copper and covered with 22-carat gold. From the tallest spire it seems to trumpet the dawning of a brighter day.

*The dome-shape idea was credited
to Brigham Young. An unverified account
claims that he took a hard-boiled egg to a meeting,
cracked it lengthwise, saying,
"I want the building shaped like that."*

The Tabernacle

When the Mormon pioneers first gazed on the Great Salt Lake desert it is unlikely they envisioned creating one of the most remarkable buildings in the world. The historic, silver-domed Salt Lake Tabernacle is a monument to their pioneer resourcefulness and is the oldest building on Temple Square. In 1971, the American Society of Civil Engineers named it a national civil engineering landmark, the first building in the United States to receive this distinction.

"Right here, we want to build a Tabernacle to accommodate the saints at our general conference and religious worship that will comfortably seat some 10,000 people," announced a counselor to Brigham Young in 1863. The magnitude of his proposal—to build an auditorium larger than most in the nation—seemed impossible. Yet, the pioneers willingly accepted the challenge.

This acceptance meant that simultaneously they would construct two prominent buildings in size and architectural design on Temple Square. The great Tabernacle was to be a place for religious assembly and the Temple, a house of the Lord, where sacred ordinances would be performed for members of the Church.

SHAPING THE ROOF

The most difficult task they encountered was creating a self-supporting roof with an unobstructed view of the pulpit. The dome-shape idea was credited to Brigham Young. An unverified account claims that he took a hard-boiled egg to a meeting, cracked it lengthwise, and placed the hollowed-out portion on a table, saying, "I want the building shaped like that." Another account bases the shape of the roof on his comment, "From

JOHN P. GEORGE

◀ **To enhance the interior beauty of the** Tabernacle, the pioneers creatively hand-finished the benches to appear like fine-grained oak and the pine pillars to resemble elegant marble. These strong pillars support a spacious "U"-shaped gallery that seats 3,000 people.

the best sounding board in the world, the roof of my mouth."

Despite irregular architectural concepts, the cornerstone was laid for the great Tabernacle on July 26, 1864, five years before the joining of the railroads in the West. Construction moved forward rapidly. Red sandstone quarried in Red Butte Canyon was used to create the foundation, the walls, and 44 supporting columns. Ox teams hauled nearly one and a half million feet of hand-cut lumber from the Wasatch Canyons. Hand-hammered metal scraps from worn-out wagon wheels were used to make nails, wooden dowels pegged together helped hold the trusses, and green rawhide wrapped around cracked timbers held the lattice arches.

Hundreds of volunteers labored to create the architectural wonder. One reporter quipped about those on the roof, "Men looking from a distance about the size of children's dolls are seen moving about on the top. We admire their nerve but could not emulate it."

As outside construction neared completion, artisans busily created beauty inside the Tabernacle. White native pine pillars were hand-finished to resemble marble, and pine benches were crafted to look like aged oak. After three years, on October 6, 1867, the doors of the great tabernacle opened to the public. A counselor to Brigham Young remarked, "I have seen a great many people assembled out of doors, but never have I seen so many in one house before!"

The acoustics in the Tabernacle were so fine that Young requested that "the crowd keep their feet still," suggesting that "the men wear Indian rubber shoes so they didn't create a lot of floor noise that conflicted with the speaker." Even today the acoustics are so sensitive that a sheet of paper torn or a pin dropped near the organ can be heard 170 feet away.

Today the Tabernacle is used by The Church of Jesus Christ of Latter-day Saints for conferences that are broadcast worldwide over radio, television, and satellite. It is best known as the home of the famous Mormon Tabernacle Choir and Organ.

THE TABERNACLE CHOIR

One month after the pioneers entered the Salt Lake Valley, choir rehearsals began. Hymns of praise from "the Crossroads of the West" have resounded from Temple Square ever since. The fame of the Mormon Tabernacle Choir has spread from land to land. Its varied and extensive repertoire and the quality of its renditions create for

PATRICK CONE

▲ *The Mormon pioneers built two remarkable buildings in a barren desert. Both are monuments to their resourcefulness and are reminiscent of an ancient day when Moses prepared a tabernacle and King Solomon directed the building of a temple in Jerusalem. The Tabernacle on Temple Square was completed in 1867, and the Temple in 1893. Both buildings are world famous for their architectural design and the purpose they fulfill at the Square.*

◁ *The widely* acclaimed Mormon Tabernacle Choir has thrilled audiences since 1847. Their weekly broadcast of "Music and the Spoken Word" from the crossroads of the West is the oldest, continual nationwide program. The choir sings sacred hymns and choral arrangements to the delight of audiences at Temple Square and throughout the world. Their most famous musical rendition is "The Battle Hymn of the Republic." From this anthem and their performances at presidential inauguration ceremonies, the choir is dubbed, "America's Choir."

millions of regular listeners a musical enjoyment unmatched anywhere in the world. The expectation of excellent performances is met each week by the 325 melodious choral voices.

Choir members volunteer their time and talents, performing each recital and broadcast without compensation. Membership in the choir requires not only a love of music but the enthusiasm of a volunteer and the discipline of a professional. Fifteen to twenty hours a week are spent rehearsing or performing in concert locally. They also travel to distant countries such as the former Soviet Union to share their musical talents. Choir President Wendell M. Smoot recognizes the sacrifices of choir members: "Some miss work opportunities when they go on tour...I think a lot of people would be quite surprised to find out just what it takes to be in the Tabernacle Choir."

From their weekly, nationwide broadcasts of "Music and the Spoken Word," and their stirring rendition of "The Battle Hymn of the Republic," has come the nickname *America's Choir*. The Mormon Tabernacle choral arrangements have thrilled audiences at four presidential inaugurations, and continue to delight visitors at Temple Square on Sunday mornings and Thursday evenings. Their rehearsals and performances are always free to the public at Temple Square.

In November 1988, the Mormon Tabernacle Choir received national recognition from the Freedom's Foundation at Valley Forge: "We salute one of America's great institutions, a magnificent group of musicians, that for years and years has stood for patriotism, love of God, and love of country."

▲ **The Tabernacle Organ and the Mormon Tabernacle Choir are as famous as the building in which** they perform. The organ was originally built by Joseph H. Ridges, an organ builder in England and Australia. He traveled to Boston to study the most sensational instrument of its day in the Boston Music Hall, hoping to learn how to create such an organ in the frontiers of the West. His ingenuity and expertise worked together to form one of the finest instruments in the world. Choir members, often accompanied by the Tabernacle organist, share their love of music and contribute their time and talents without compensation. They sing songs of praise that uplift and bring joy to countless millions. Organ recitals and choir performances are free to the public at Temple Square.

The Tabernacle Organ

In 1867 Brigham Young declared, "We cannot preach the Gospel unless we have good music. I am waiting patiently for the organ to be finished. Then we can sing the Gospel into the hearts of the people."

The story of building the Tabernacle Organ is an epic of creativity and perseverance. Straight-grained wood from Pine Valley in southern Utah was used to create the pipes and console by organ builder, Joseph H. Ridges. Glue was made by boiling homemade batches in large pots, nails were created from hand-hammered metal scraps, while strong rope was made from pelts and rawhide. Every facet of the great organ was the product of pioneer industry.

In 1869 one visitor exclaimed, "A remarkable piece of mechanism to be built in this country, and that it is not inferior so far as completed, to the eastern and foreign made articles of its class."

The organ was first powered by hand pumping the bellows. The pumping mechanism so exhausted its operators, that within a half hour new recruits were needed. A humorous incident occurred between one of the organists and the bellows operators during a recital. The organist, overly concerned with pleasing important visitors in the audience, displayed inward tension by curt and prideful remarks to the operators. Angered by his comments they failed to pump the organ when he tried to play. After the organist reprimanded the leader, he retorted, "Well, I just wanted you to remember, and our dignified guests to know, that there was someone else beside you who had something to do with the working of the organ."

The pumping mechanism was replaced by a large water wheel and later by electrical power. Many of the original wooden pipes, however, are still used. The 11,623 pipes vary in size from three-fourths of an inch to 32 feet tall. The 206 ranks or sets of pipes are operated by adjusting the knobs on either side of the five manual keyboards.

The magnificent sounds of serenity, grandeur, and power emanating from the Tabernacle Organ has led eminent organ authorities to proclaim this instrument one of the finest in the world. Organ recitals are held daily and are free to the public.

SUGGESTED READING

GROW, STEWART L. *A Tabernacle in the Desert.* Salt Lake City, Utah: Deseret Book Company, 1958.

OWEN, BARBARA. *The Mormon Tabernacle Organ: An American Classic.* Available at the Museum of Church History and Art in Salt Lake City, Utah.

◀ *The Tabernacle interior, reminiscent of past eras with antique chandeliers and wooden pipes, provides a feeling of historic grandeur. The tall, rounded pipes are covered with gold leaf and are still used by prominent organists in daily recitals at Temple Square. The pipes range in size from 32-feet-tall to less than one inch. Many renowned organists claim the Tabernacle Organ is one of the world's greatest instruments. Visitors to Temple Square agree.*

The building of the Tabernacle Organ ▷ *is an epic of creativity and perseverance. Diligent pioneer workmanship resulted in a superb musical tone that now emanates from 206 sets of organ pipes. The sound produced is controlled by the "push or pull of a button" on the side of the organ console. Thus, an organist can create the desired volume and tone for each musical recital.*

JOHN P. GEORGE

JOHN P. GEORGE

▲ *The nearness of the vertical Temple spires to the silver-domed Tabernacle lends contrasting beauty to Temple Square. The Tabernacle roof is recognized as one of the greatest works of timber framing in the world. Henry Grow, architect and former bridge builder, is credited with creating the contrasting architectural marvel.*

PATRICK CONE

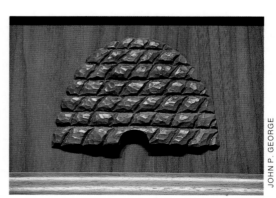

JOHN P. GEORGE

▲ *The hand-carved beehive on the Tabernacle podium is a symbol of Mormon pioneer industry.*

◄ *Red sandstone quarried in Red Butte Canyon, located near Salt Lake City, was used in building the foundation and columns for the Tabernacle.*

***M**any of the* ▶ *original wooden pipes brought by ox team from Pine Valley in southern Utah are still used in the Tabernacle Organ today. The elliptical shape of the tabernacle roof causes the sound produced by the pipes to bounce from every chair as it vibrates throughout the building. The wooden pipes and the structure of the building combine to form acoustical qualities that have made this organ world famous.*

JOHN P. GEORGE

***Overleaf:** The world-traveling Mormon Tabernacle Choir is nowhere better than at Temple Square. Photo by John P. George.*

*Expressions of peaceful happiness
are often heard sprinkled
with grateful remembrances of the
inherent religious freedoms enjoyed in America.*

In Grateful Remembrance:
Reflective Monuments

A stroll through the sequestered ten acres of Temple Square reveals the wonders of nature. Walkways dotted with hundreds of varieties of beautiful flowers, blossoming near towering shade trees, provide a botanical delight. "There is nothing like it in all the world. It is like an oasis in the desert," exclaimed one visitor. At the Christmas season this oasis reaches breathtaking heights as 300,000 miniature lights strung on trees and shrubs, walkways and walls create a joyous atmosphere to celebrate the birth of Jesus Christ.

During all seasons the Square is filled with visitors who gaze at the beauties of nature as they stroll past engraved plaques, bronze statues, and flowing fountains. Expressions of peaceful happiness are often heard sprinkled with grateful remembrances of the inherent religious freedoms enjoyed in America.

THE CLASSIC NAUVOO TEMPLE BELL

Each hour the Nauvoo Temple Bell rings as a reminder of religious freedom. The bronze bell, weighing 782 pounds, was a gift to the Mormon Church from its early British converts. Its resounding tones first emanated in Illinois from the bell tower in the Nauvoo Temple. Unfortunately, its

The Nauvoo Temple Bell, a gift from ▷ *British converts, rings hourly at Temple Square as a reminder of the religious freedom enjoyed in the United States. It peals from a bell tower, erected in honor of sisterhood, that was designed by Lorenzo S. Young, a grandson of Brigham Young.*

JOHN P. GEORGE

sounds of freedom were silenced by unruly mobs. Courageously, David Lamoureaux wrestled the bell from mobocrats and hid it in a large barrel of beans in 1846. He and his family chose to walk 1,300 miles from Nauvoo to the Salt Lake Valley so the temple bell might be secure in their wagon.

HANDCART PIONEER STATUE

The bronze statue, "The Handcart Family," is the work of Norwegian sculptor Torlief Knaphus. His art was "crafted as a monument commemorating the dedication, sacrifice, and faith of the early handcart company pioneers." It is a poignant tribute to thousands of immigrants who crossed the rugged plains seeking religious freedom nearly 150 years ago.

The National Association of Traveling Organizations lists Temple Square as a main attraction for visitors in December because of the multicolored lights adorning the Square. Three hundred thousand tiny bulbs are strung from trees, shrubs, and walls to remind visitors of the birth of Jesus Christ, who is the light of the world. Concerts by acclaimed symphonies and choruses fill the air with Christmas carols: "Silent Night, Holy Night" . . . "Oh Little Town of Bethlehem" . . . "Away in a Manger" . . . add to the festive spirit in the Square.

The statue depicts a pioneer family pushing and pulling a two-wheeled cart with their earthly possessions tied on top. Many immigrants were too poor to purchase animals and wagons, yet they still chose to make the arduous trek to the Salt Lake Valley. Levi Edgar Young, a professor of Western History at the University of Utah, stated: "They came here to find their God, and nothing could divert them from their purpose."

The new settlers colonized a parched and arid desert. Native plants similar to those growing around the handcart monument—sagebrush, rabbitbrush, greasewood, manzanita, and cactus—had to be cleared before the pioneers could transform the barren surroundings into a blossoming garden.

SEAGULL MONUMENT

In 1913, the Seagull Monument was erected on Temple Square in memory of God's mercy to the Mormon pioneers in 1848. In that year crickets began to devour the crops. Frantically, the pioneers tried to destroy the insects by burning, drowning, and even fighting them with clubs, brooms, and shovels. Despite their physical efforts the crickets continued their destruction.

With strength exhausted and hopes for a harvest dim, the pioneers prayed for relief. In answer to their plea, cries of seagulls were heard punctuating the sky. These birds consumed the crickets and became the means for saving the crops.

"The Miracle of the Gulls" created by sculptor Mahonri Young of two bronze-gilded birds with outstretched wings mounted atop a granite shaft commemorates this event. It stands as a reminder that the Lord continues to hear and answer prayers.

ASSEMBLY HALL

An architectural jewel on Temple Square is the Assembly Hall, completed in 1880. Located in the shadow of the Tabernacle, eclipsed by size and public exposure, it is a stunning favorite. The Assembly Hall is a beautiful, miniature cathedral built from the pile of leftovers originally designated for the Tabernacle and the Temple.

The designer, Obed Taylor, chose discarded sandstone from the Tabernacle for the foundation, and granite hewn in its rustic, natural state, discarded by Temple builders, for the outer walls. The texture of the building is visibly rough and contrasts with the ornamental spires 130-feet high atop the gabled roof. The varied contour creates an elegant gothic appearance.

JOHN P. GEORGE

The interior of the building is adorned with pine pews grained to resemble oak, and columns painted to appear like marble that support the horseshoe balcony. The 40 stained-glass windows cast a warm glow, while the stars of David are reminiscent of ancient Israelite origin and glory.

In 1980, a routine inspection of the Assembly Hall revealed deterioration of the large wooden trusses in the attic. Consequently, for three years the building was closed for renovation. When the doors reopened they revealed a new hardwood

▲ **A** *favorite on Temple Square is the Assembly Hall, a semi-gothic structure created from discarded*
granite blocks originally intended for the Temple. Completed in 1882, it was first used only for religious services.
Seating 1,400 people, this stately building today also features concerts and a lecture series.

floor, elaborate draperies, and a ceiling accentuated with gold-leaf designs. Three organ rehearsal rooms improved practice facilities for organists who performed on the new baroque instrument. Larger colored pipes for the organ were crafted from heat-treated copper and tin to create a clearer sound. The extensive restoration has preserved this architectural jewel to the delight of visitors.

The Assembly Hall serves as a center for renowned musicians and prominent lecturers to share their talents. Monthly program schedules of free performances and lectures are available upon request at the visitor centers.

SUGGESTED READING

RICH, RUSSELL R. *Ensign to the Nations*. Provo, Utah: Brigham Young University Publications, 1972.

◄ *The ornate doors of the* Assembly Hall best illustrate pioneer artistic detail and symbolism significant to Mormon beliefs. Jewish visitors to Temple Square are intrigued to find the Star of David over both Assembly Hall entrances. These ancient emblems are among the myriad represented in the Hall. When the gold-motif doors are opened they reveal an interior of exquisite beauty and symbolism that rivals the artistry of the outside entrances.

JOHN P. GEORGE

The pine used in the ▷ Assembly Hall was grained to resemble the oak of the organ, and the tall columns supporting the horseshoe balcony painted to simulate marble. The ornate chandeliers suspend from a decorative ceiling accentuated with gold leaf. This added beauty is another evidence of early pioneer culture and refinement often seen in other structures in the Great Salt Lake Valley.

JOHN P. GEORGE

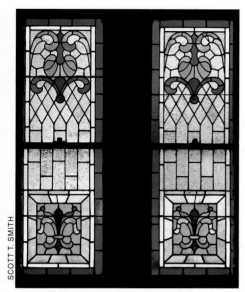

▲ **F**orty stained glass
windows cast a warm glow over
the interior of the Assembly Hall.

The Assembly Hall, like a carriage ▷
ride, is reminiscent of another era—an era
unencumbered by traffic and noise—a
simpler time, a time of quiet, shared joy.

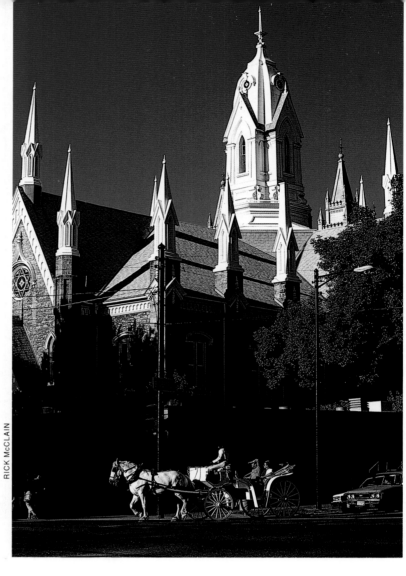

◁ **T**he baroque-
style organ is a fully
encased classical
instrument. Its
decorative oak carvings
were created to unify
with other features in the
Assembly Hall. Symbols
meaningful to the
Mormon culture, like the
beehive and the sego
lily, the Utah state flower,
are carved into
the panels.

◀ *The Seagull Monument was sculpted by Mahonri Young and* ▲ *memorializes God's mercy to the Mormon pioneers in 1848. In answer to prayer, a myriad of seagulls devoured hoards of crickets that were destroying the pioneers' crops. This incident is referred to as the "Miracle of the Gulls." The seagull has become the state bird of Utah and this statue, the only known monument erected to honor a bird, symbolically portrays the Lord hears and answers prayers.*

▼ **T**he Handcart Monument was created to remember the many pioneers who crossed the plains in the 1850s pushing and pulling their possessions in wooden handcarts. These pioneers were too poor to acquire oxen and wagons, yet with unyielding courage trekked to the Rocky Mountains seeking religious freedom. The story of their hardships as they walked to the Salt Lake Valley is unequaled in pioneering history. Many lost their lives in heavy snows, while others were maimed by frostbite, and yet desire to worship the Lord in freedom propelled survivors to move forward. This monument, surrounded by the desert plants native to the valley, stands on Temple Square as an example of those who possess courage amid affliction. The monument was unveiled on September 25, 1926, on the Square.

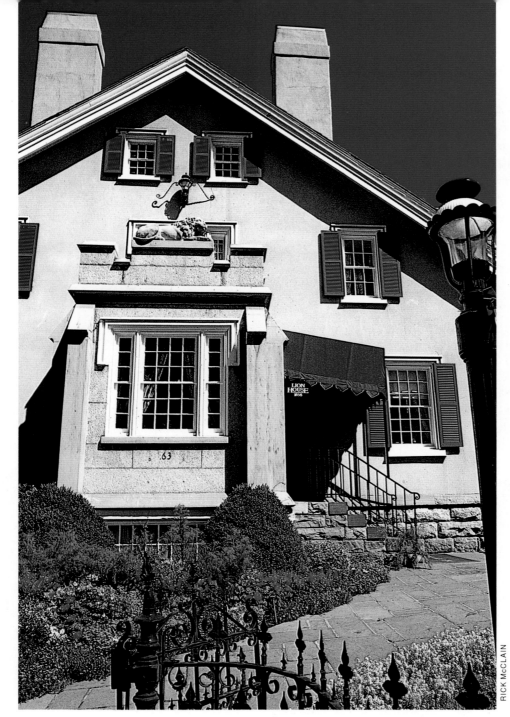

◄ **Near Temple Square is the** Lion House, built in 1856. This gabled structure was once part of Brigham Young's home, which included the colonial style Beehive House that served as his principal residence from 1854 to 1877. It was in these two homes that Brigham reared his children and entertained dignitaries from throughout the nation. The Lion House was designed by William Ward, and named for the stone lion he sculpted on the front porch. To the architect the lion was symbolic of Brigham Young, who was often referred to as "the Lion of the Lord." The Lion House, restored with elegant furnishings from the pioneer era, now serves as a social center for private reservation banquets. A pantry in the renovated home is open to the public during the lunch hour.

RICK McCLAIN

PATRICK CONE

◄ **The winding walks of Temple Square** reveal not only beautiful gardens and shade trees, but unique designs that convey a pictorial message. This design illustrates the worldwide interest of Mormons in extending friendship and goodwill to all people and cultures regardless of their beliefs and ideologies.

Life-size statues of
Joseph Smith and his brother, Hyrum, were created by sculptor Mahonri Young. They are a reminder that these men sealed their testimony of the truthfulness of the Book of Mormon on June 27, 1844, at Carthage, Illinois. The Prophet Joseph Smith declared, "I shall die innocent, and it shall yet be said of me—he was murdered in cold blood."

JOHN P. GEORGE

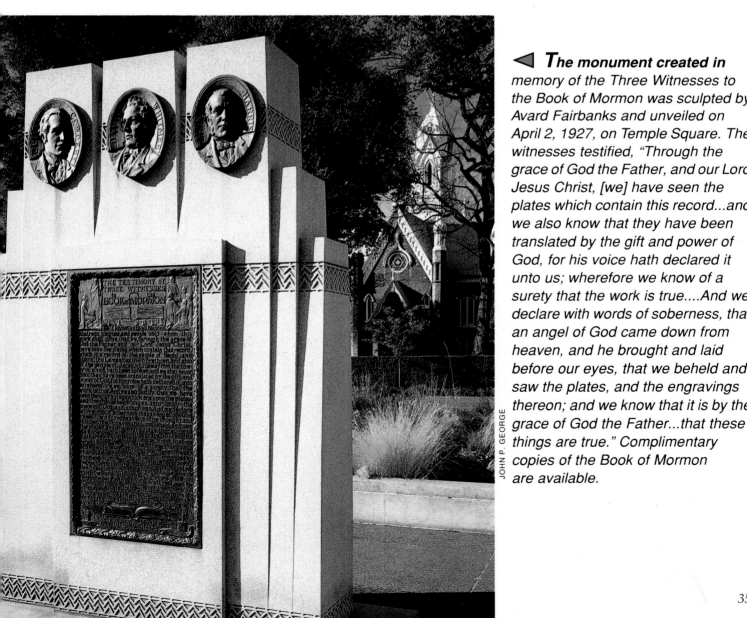

◀ *The monument created in* memory of the Three Witnesses to the Book of Mormon was sculpted by Avard Fairbanks and unveiled on April 2, 1927, on Temple Square. The witnesses testified, "Through the grace of God the Father, and our Lord Jesus Christ, [we] have seen the plates which contain this record...and we also know that they have been translated by the gift and power of God, for his voice hath declared it unto us; wherefore we know of a surety that the work is true....And we declare with words of soberness, that an angel of God came down from heaven, and he brought and laid before our eyes, that we beheld and saw the plates, and the engravings thereon; and we know that it is by the grace of God the Father...that these things are true." Complimentary copies of the Book of Mormon are available.

JOHN P. GEORGE

*F*ew monuments touch the heartstrings
of visitors more than this beautiful,
impressive 12-foot statue of Jesus Christ.
He stands symbolically in the middle
of the universe as the Creator of the World.

A Haven of Peace

Temple Square, located in the heart of downtown Salt Lake City, is the number one tourist attraction in Utah. "In no other city does a tourist out for a good time devote so much time to religion as in Salt Lake City," penned a reporter for the *St. Louis Star*.

The Square is open to the public daily from 8:00 a.m. to 10:00 a.m. June through August, and from 9:00 a.m. to 9:00 p.m. September through May. Guides with foreign language skills are available and tours can be arranged for those on tight schedules. Free guided tours, organ recitals, and concerts are available throughout the day.

Two visitor centers located on the north and south of the Square display inspiring exhibits—murals, paintings, statues, dioramas, movies and other visual displays—that introduce the tourist to the origins and beliefs of The Church of Jesus Christ of Latter-day Saints, with added emphasis on the importance of family unity.

SOUTH VISITOR CENTER

In the South Visitor Center artistic renderings of scenes from the Book of Mormon adorn the building. It is from this book that The Church of Jesus Christ of Latter-day Saints gets its nickname, "Mormons." Church members regard the Book of Mormon and the Holy Bible as companion scriptures, both testifying of Jesus Christ.

Highlighted within the center is a large baptismal font resting on the backs of 12 oxen that symbolically represent the 12 tribes of Israel. Also featured are lighted pictures of the interior of the Salt Lake Temple and a diorama history of the early beginnings of the Mormon church. A short video presentation of the Book of Mormon and the purpose of temples can also be seen.

JOHN P. GEORGE

◄ **The joy a mother and her children find in** being together need not end at death. Latter-day Saints believe that through sacred ordinances performed in a Temple, beautiful family relationships can be eternal. "For behold, this is my work and my glory—to bring to pass the immortality and eternal life of man" (Moses 1:39).

▲ *The marble replica of Bertel Thorvaldsen's Christus is the highlight of the North Visitor Center.*
Sidney King painted the universe on the walls and ceiling of the rotunda room as a background for the Christus
reproduced by Aldo Rebachi of Florence, Italy. Their shared talents dramatically
remind the visitor that Christ is the Creator of the universe, the Savior of the world. ▼

NORTH VISITOR CENTER

Well-known and respected artists created illustrations of biblical themes for the center. Their inspiring display forms a pictorial gallery that spans throughout the building. It begins with a statue of Adam and Eve and moves to large murals of Noah, Abraham, Moses, and Daniel.

The focal point of the artistic renderings is found in the spacious rotunda room where, amid the ceiling mural of the universe is "The Christus," a replica of the immortal masterpiece sculpted by Bertel Thorvaldsen and located in Copenhagen, Denmark.

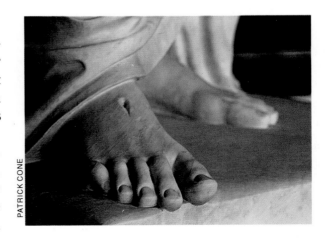

PATRICK CONE

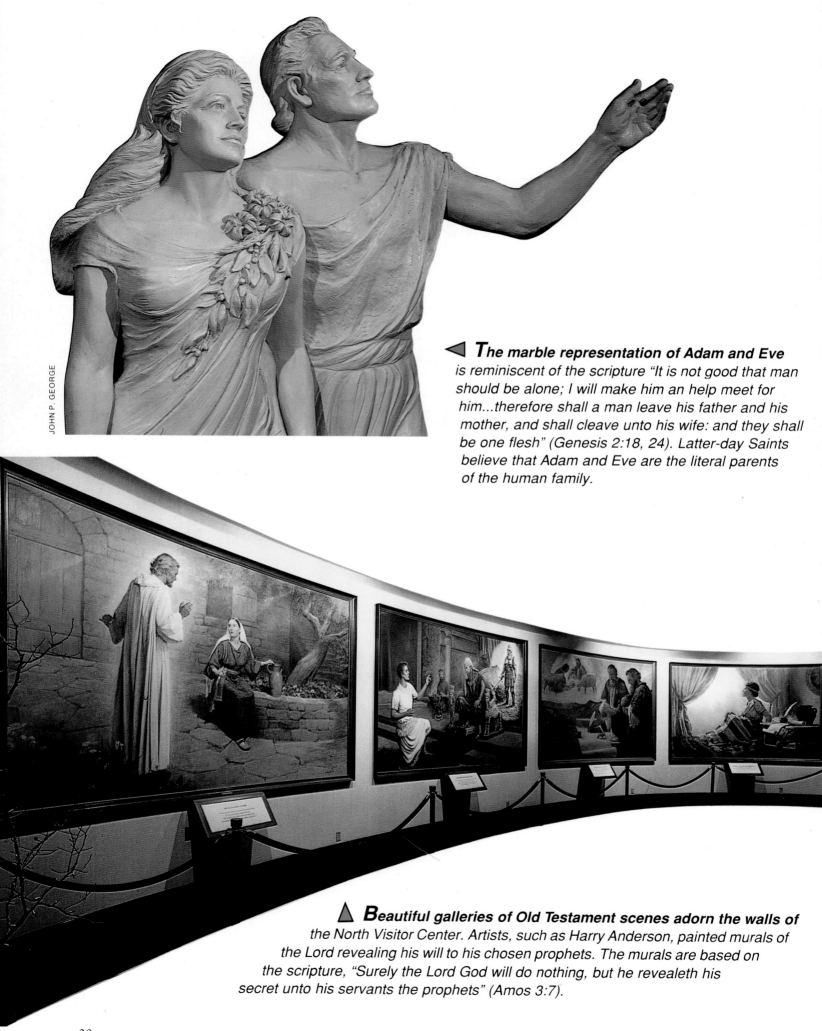

JOHN P. GEORGE

◀ **The marble representation of Adam and Eve** is reminiscent of the scripture "It is not good that man should be alone; I will make him an help meet for him...therefore shall a man leave his father and his mother, and shall cleave unto his wife: and they shall be one flesh" (Genesis 2:18, 24). Latter-day Saints believe that Adam and Eve are the literal parents of the human family.

▲ **Beautiful galleries of Old Testament scenes adorn the walls of** the North Visitor Center. Artists, such as Harry Anderson, painted murals of the Lord revealing his will to his chosen prophets. The murals are based on the scripture, "Surely the Lord God will do nothing, but he revealeth his secret unto his servants the prophets" (Amos 3:7).

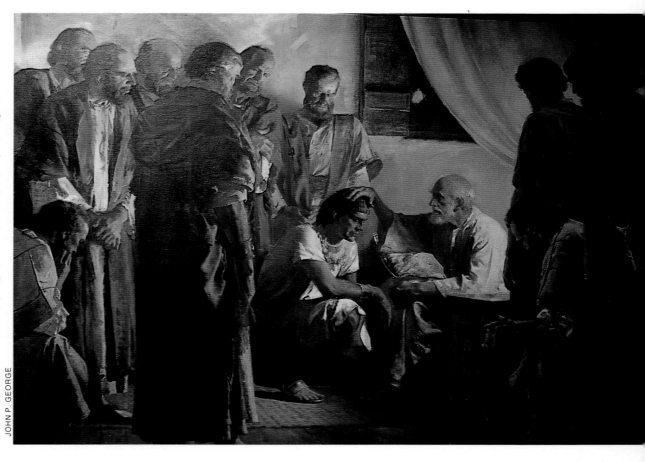

Near the end of ▷ *Jacob's life, he gathered his twelve sons together to give them a father's blessing, a blessing for the house of Israel. The patriarch Jacob, known as Israel, blessed his sons and their posterity. He admonished them to keep the commandments and prophesied of events that would occur in the latter days.*

JOHN P. GEORGE

JOHN P. GEORGE

◁ *The Lord made a covenant with faithful Abraham, promising him that he would be the father of many nations and "all the nations of the earth shall be blessed in him" (Genesis 18:18). This promise or Abrahamic Covenant began to be fulfilled when Sarah gave birth to a son named Isaac. The artist's portrayal of Abraham alone with only his staff for support contrasts with the promise he soon received that he would have posterity and would be viewed as a great patriarch by many nations.*

◀ **Chronological** vignettes of the life of Jesus Christ are displayed in a series of murals in the North Visitor Center. A favorite for many visitors is the mural of Christ praying in the Garden of Gesthemane. They are reminded of Matthew 26:39: "O my Father, if it be possible, let this cup pass from me: nevertheless not as I will, but as thou wilt." His willingness to atone for sins and to give His life is an act of love, for "Greater love hath no man than this, that a man lay down his life for his friends" (John 15:13).

HARRY JARVIS

SCOTT T. SMITH

▲ **The painting of the resurrected Christ instructing his disciples to "Go ye** therefore, and teach all nations, baptizing them in the name of the Father, and of the Son, and of the Holy Ghost" (Matthew 28:19), was created by Harry Anderson. A large replica by Grant Clawson is located in the lobby of the Church Office Building.

◀ **A baptismal** font resting on the backs of 12 oxen is displayed in the South Visitor Center. In similar fonts located within Latter-day Saint Temples, baptisms are performed vicariously for the deceased. The apostle Paul penned: "Else what shall they do which are baptized for the dead, if the dead rise not at all? why are they then baptized for the dead?" (First Corinthians 15:29).

JOHN P. GEORGE

JOHN P. GEORGE

▲ **A three-dimensional diorama featuring the early beginnings of The Church of Jesus Christ of** Latter-day Saints, with emphasis on the coming forth of the Book of Mormon is located in the South Visitor Center. The Book of Mormon is a record of ancient inhabitants who lived in the Americas.

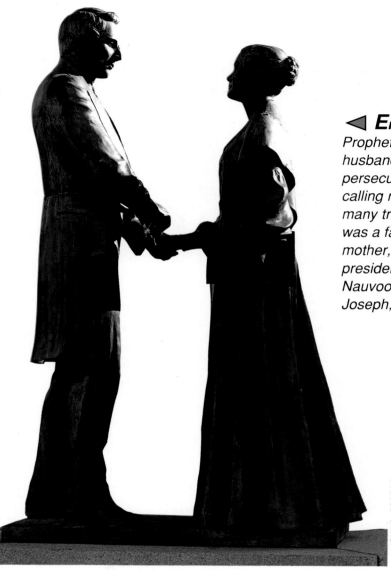

◄ **Emma Smith, the wife of the** Prophet Joseph Smith, stood next to her husband during years of extreme persecution. Her belief in his prophetic calling remained strong despite the many trials she also endured. Emma was a faithful companion, a loving mother, and served as the first president of the Relief Society in Nauvoo. Her last words were, "Joseph, Joseph, Joseph."

JOHN P. GEORGE

ful, impressive 12-foot statue of Jesus Christ. He stands symbolically in the middle of the universe as the Creator of the World.

After viewing "The Christus," visitors are then invited to gaze upon New Testament murals of Christ. Biblical scenes of Jesus teaching in the Temple, his baptism, and his selection of the disciples are artistic masterpieces that create a spirit of reverence in the center.

One tourist found more than a renewal of feelings for the divine. "Will you tell me how to produce a young man like that?" he said pointing to his guide. For him, the personality of his guide was the highlight of the tour. For others it is the visual displays of peace and the moments they reflected on the Son of God. For all, regardless of age, race, religion, or position in life, it is comforting to know that there is still a haven of peace to be enjoyed every day at Temple Square.

SUGGESTED READING

TALMAGE, JAMES E. *Jesus The Christ.* Salt Lake City, Utah: Deseret Book Company, 1962.
The Book of Mormon. Salt Lake City, Utah: The Church of Jesus Christ of Latter-day Saints, 1989.

PATRICK CONE

▲ **The 8 million yearly visitors to Temple** Square are delighted to learn that tours are not only free but available in several languages.

▲ **The Mormon pioneers wanted the buildings and surroundings at Temple Square to reflect their** quiet reverence for the Lord. With care and craftsmanship they constructed the buildings and the grounds. With that same care, Christmas lights are strung today to highlight the ornate construction and the gardens. Christmas lights do not adorn the buildings because of their nature and uniqueness.

▲ *East of Temple Square is the modern 28-story Church Office Building erected in 1972. General* authorities of The Church of Jesus Christ of Latter-day Saints have offices within the building as do many organizational leaders. Tours of the office building include a visit to the historical department and an unforgettable view of the Salt Lake Valley from the top floor.

Members of the Church currently number 8 million worldwide. Many of these members are examples of the Savior's teaching, "That ye love one another; as I have loved you" (John 13:34). They extend love to neighbors both home and abroad. Ethiopia, Somalia, Romania, and other far-reaches of the world have benefitted from their humanitarian assistance. Victims of floods, hurricanes, and earthquakes within the United States have also received assistance. The Church of Jesus Christ of Latter-day Saints reaches out as did the Good Samaritan to those in need and extends an invitation to "Come unto Christ." The worldwide influence for good has given hope to the downtrodden and love to the forgotten.

SOUTH VISITOR CENTER

ASSEMBLY HALL

TABERNACLE

TEMPLE

TEMPLE ANNEX

NORTH VISITOR CENTER

PATRICK CONE

▲ **Temple Square in Salt Lake City, is Utah's number one tourist attraction. Whether to see the** Tabernacle, the Temple, the Assembly Hall, the Visitor Centers, or the botanical gardens, visitors fill the Square each day. Many enjoy free concert series, organ recitals, and choir rehearsals of the famous Mormon Tabernacle Choir. Others spend reflective moments away from the traffic and noise of our modern society. Each finds at Temple Square valuable memories not soon forgotten.

The enclosed ten acres that comprise Salt Lake City's world-renowned Temple Square, are home to some of the most readily recognized and architecturally honored buildings in existence today.

The oldest building in the Square is the Tabernacle. The cornerstone was laid in 1864 and, through the efforts of hundreds of volunteer laborers, the doors opened to the public in just three years —on October 6, 1867. It was not only the largest auditorium in the nation, its innovative shape and dome roof were architectural wonders.

In 1880, the Assembly Hall was completed allowing the public access to a miniature cathedral built from granite boulders left over from construction of the Temple. Featuring well-known musicians and lecturers, the programs offered are well received by the 8 million annual visitors to Temple Square.

The foundation for the Temple was begun in 1853, and the sacred edifice—closed to the public—was completed 40 years later in 1893.

Although close in proximity and constructed at the same time, the Temple spires contrast dramatically with the dome-shaped Tabernacle.

A glorious past symbolizes devotion, faith, and courage.

To look back at Temple Square and the beauty that was created in the barren desert of the Salt Lake Valley is to remember a glorious past. Not a past without heart-ache, disappointment, or death, but a past that symbolizes the best of devotion, faith, and courage. The example of the Mormon pioneers is remembered not only for what they achieved in their native surroundings, but also for the manner they chose to "wear out their lives." They literally gave their all to enjoy religious freedom. Their search for freedom to worship extended from New York to the Salt Lake Valley. Reflecting upon their sacrifice strengthens our faith and heightens our courage. The Mormon pioneers left more than buildings—they left their lives as a hope for a better world.

"**T**hou shalt love the Lord thy ▷
God...love thy neighbour as thyself"
(Matthew 22:37, 39).

JOHN P. GEORGE

Books on national park areas in "The Story Behind the Scenery" series are: Acadia, Alcatraz Island, Arches, Big Bend, Biscayne, Blue Ridge Parkway, Bryce Canyon, Canyon de Chelly, Canyonlands, Cape Cod, Capitol Reef, Channel Islands, Civil War Parks, Colonial, Crater Lake, Death Valley, Denali, Devils Tower, Dinosaur, Everglades, Fort Clatsop, Gettysburg, Glacier, Glen Canyon-Lake Powell, Grand Canyon, Grand Canyon-North Rim, Grand Teton, Great Basin, Great Smoky Mountains, Haleakala, Hawaii Volcanoes, Independence, Lake Mead-Hoover Dam, Lassen Volcanic, Lincoln Parks, Mammoth Cave, Mesa Verde, Mount Rainier, Mount Rushmore, National Park Service, National Seashores, North Cascades, Olympic, Petrified Forest, Redwood, Rocky Mountain, Scotty's Castle, Sequoia & Kings Canyon, Shenandoah, Statue of Liberty, Theodore Roosevelt, Virgin Islands, Yellowstone, Yosemite, Zion.

Additional books in "The Story Behind the Scenery" series are: Annapolis, Big Sur, Colorado Plateau, Columbia River Gorge, Fire: A Force of Nature, Grand Circle Adventure, John Wesley Powell, Kauai, Lake Tahoe, Las Vegas, Lewis & Clark, Monument Valley, Mormon Temple Square, Mormon Trail, Mount St. Helens, Nevada's Red Rock Canyon, Nevada's Valley of Fire, Oregon Trail, Oregon Trail Center, Santa Catalina, Santa Fe Trail, Sharks, Sonoran Desert, U.S. Virgin Islands, Water: A Gift of Nature, Whales.

A companion series of national park areas is the NEW "in pictures...The Continuing Story." This series has **Translation Packages**, providing each title with a complete text both in English and, individually, a second language, German, French, or Japanese. Selected titles in both this series and our other books are available in up to five additional languages. **Call (800-626-9673), fax (702-433-3420), or write to the address below.**

Published by KC Publications, 3245 E. Patrick Ln., Suite A, Las Vegas, NV 89120

Inside back cover: The Angel Moroni as seen at night. Photo by Rick McClain.

Back cover: Golden leaves of locust trees frame the east face of the Temple. Photo by John P. George.

Created, Designed and Published in the U.S.A.
Printed by Dong-A Publishing and Printing, Seoul, Korea
Color Separations by Kedia/Kwangyangsa Co., Ltd.